Sunny's Heart

By **Na'ama Gal**

Illustrations by **Marika Mihalache**

Sunny's Heart

Written by **Na'ama Gal**

Illustrated by **Marika Mihalache**

Translated by **Dana Translators**

Edited by **Tal Ifergan**

Graphics by **Simple Story**

Copyright © 2020 by Na'ama Gal

All rights reserved. No part of this book may be used or reproduced in any matter whatsoever without permission in writing from the author except in the case of brief quotations embodied in critical articles or reviews.

First edition 2020

simplestory
Digital Publishing

To my four children and their beloved partners, and to my three grandchildren: Roni, Yarden and Ben, who fill my heart with endless joy and love

Sunny is a smiley, happy child.
As bright as the sun,
so shines his smile.

Sunny loves to have fun and laugh all day,
to jump, roll around and run far away.

He loves playing with his sister, Emily
with his friends and family;
and also loves singing and racing,
long walks, and butterfly chasing.

But sometimes things happen to Sunny
that make him feel emotions
That aren't at all nice and funny.

Because Sunny can feel everything,
large or small,
since his heart is **so big**, it can feel it all.

One day, when Sunny was outside
playing with his toys,
all of a sudden, he heard a loud noise.
He was frightened and felt his heart aching
and stood still at once, shaking.

He took some deep breaths, quite a few,
and stood there silently, for a moment or two.

   Daddy hugged him and lovingly said:
   "You got scared for a minute,
   and that made you feel bad."

Because Sunny can feel everything,
large or small,
since his heart is **so big**,
it can feel it all.

Sunny calmed down, feeling happy and cool.
He climbed up the ladder,
and jumped into the pool.

One day, Sunny and his sister
played with his toy plane.
They flew it up in the air, took it apart,
and assembled it back again.

Suddenly, the plane crashed
and broke into pieces.

Emily was startled, she felt bad,
and Sunny was crying loud,
he was sad.

Mom embraced Sunny and whispered,
nodding her head:
"It's important to cry when you're sad.
You get rid of the bad feelings,
and again, feel glad."

Emily gave them a timid smile,
and Sunny continued crying for a little while.
Until he no longer needed to vent
and was back to feeling content.

Sunny then stood up happily and stated:
"I'll build a new airplane now,
big and fast so you'll say 'wow!'"

Because Sunny can feel everything,
large or small,
since his heart is so big, it can feel it all.

Sunny came to visit his friend, Jay,
at his home one day.
But Jay wanted on his own to play,
without making Sunny feel welcome to stay.

Sunny became angry, and in a raised,
loud voice he said:
"Stop behaving like this,
you're not being a friend!"

Though a little offended, Jay tried to explain:
"I was worried that something
would happen to my brand-new game.

"I'm sorry, Sunny, I love you,
I really do.
I want, very much, to be a good friend to you!"

Sunny was excited and hugged Jay,
and just like that, their fight was over,
and they went to play.

Sunny's heart was once again
joyful and glad,
after yelling, crying and
being angry and sad.

He rolled around on the grass,
and played with his friends.
Planted some flowers in the garden,
and ran all over with a smile
that never ends.

Because Sunny can feel everything,
large or small,
since his heart is **so big**,
it can feel it all.

At night,
mommy read Sunny a story.
But Sunny felt it was boring,
and started shifting around, yawning,
laughing and snoring.

"If you're bored," mommy said with a soft gaze,
"you can choose another game:
Lego, a puzzle, maybe even a maze.

Boredom has a secret, did you know?
it helps you find out what you want,
what you love so!"

Mommy is still talking,
but the room's door is already ajar...
Sunny is running around,
laughing and spreading love and joy -
just like a star.

Because Sunny can feel everything,
large or small,
since his heart is **so big**, it can feel it all.

The sun was shining and the family went out
for a happy stroll.
Mommy then told Sunny how wonderful it is
that he understands emotions
without any confusion at all.

"You understood that
there are no 'bad' or 'good' emotions,
and that they all have important roles to play,
so, there is no reason to keep any of them at bay.

Out of your body, you let your feelings flow,
and don't leave them inside,
to take up more room and grow."

Sunny listened to his mom
and said, with a grin:
"The body helps the heart relax
and ease the pain within.
So that I - just like my name,
can be happy, calm, and shine
with joy, once again!

Dear parents,

The story "Sunny's Heart" is about emotions.
In our natural state, we feel joy, serenity, satisfaction, contentment and love.
Sometimes we experience painful emotions. This is normal.
Each painful emotion is released from our bodies in its own unique way: through trembling, laughter, crying or yelling.
It is important to provide our children with the freedom and confidence to express their emotions the natural way (even if sometimes it annoys, offends or bothers us, the parents).

Every emotion plays a role in our lives, and all emotions are important for our health, functioning and development.
Each painful emotion that is fully released from the body can help us—

fear can turn into a driving force, which encourages us to make some sort of change for the better.
Sadness can help us separate from "the old" (an object to which we were attached, such as Sunny's toy airplane; a place where we lived or worked; a person we knew and loved), and tap into tranquility and gentleness, to joy and to hope.
Anger gives us the courage to express our real emotions and solve problems that bother us.
Boredom can help us discover our real desire, and connect to what truly excites and fulfills us.

It is important to direct our children towards doing new things which are good for them, once they had released the painful emotions and calmed down.
This way the children can quickly and rapidly return to being happy, content and serene.

There Are No "Good" Emotions or "Bad" Emotions

We have been taught that we are only allowed to experience "good" emotions (love, compassion, empathy, joy, serenity etc.), and that we should suppress and hide the "bad" emotions (such as fear, stress, jealousy, anger, sadness, and frustration).

Why?

Because "we have to be strong, brave and polite, and adjust ourselves to our parents and to society". However, our stubborn struggle with our "bad" emotions (which surface naturally when we experience something unpleasant), and our attempts at hiding them are, in fact, what make it difficult for us and rob us from our serenity and joy.

If you hold back your children from expressing their emotions (through body language, verbally, behaviorally or in any other way), the painful emotions will remain locked inside their bodies and will not disappear. They might erupt suddenly, without prior indication, without control and very forcefully, or rather remain in the body for many years, harming it.

Activities with children

Activities which help the children relate to their emotions and release painful feelings from their bodies, in full, without hurting anyone else:

1. What is the emotion called?

An activity designed to teach children the names of the emotions, and to identify which emotions are pleasant and which are not.

Below is a recommended list of emotions of all kinds, according to the child's age, stage of development and personality:

Pleasant Emotions

Joy; Love; Serenity; Confidence; Forgiveness; Hope; Gratitude;
Pride; Relief; Admiration; Satisfaction; Enjoyment; Gratification; Lightness;
Curiosity; Enthusiasm; Cheerfulness; Caring; Excitement; Affection; Appreciation

Unpleasant Emotions

Apprehension; Longing; Guilt; Concern; Anger; Embarrassment; Fright;
Revenge; Insult; Fear; Boredom; Disrespect; Regret; Confusion;
Shame; Disappointment; Tiredness; Agitation; Sadness; Remorse; Stress

Knowing what the emotions are called helps the children identify what they are feeling.

If they can express their feelings and let them out of their bodies, they will avoid doing things they might regret later on, such as committing acts during fits of rage.

If a child recognizes a rush of great anger inside himself, he would be able to say to his friend, exercising complete self-control: "I'm very angry at what you've done!" rather than hit him.

2. What does the heart feel?

Make sure to ask your children, on different occasions, what they are feeling in their hearts and bodies. This inwards reflection is very important. One must practice identifying and naming emotions, in order to raise awareness to the emotion that is surfacing, and to be able to express how it feels in words.

3. Let the children in on what you are feeling...

Set a personal example for sharing emotions. Encourage the children, out of honesty and closeness, to express their own emotions as well.

For example, let us say you returned home from work angry, because a co-worker said unpleasant things to you, with which you do not agree. Share what had happened with the children and let them know that you are angry, offended, stressed or disappointed by this instance.

4. Who can guess what?

Play with your children a game where each participant displays a certain emotion, and the others need to figure out what it is.

Learning through experience and play is very significant.

While the children practice expressing emotions, you will get to spend some fun quality time with them.

5. Do not offend!

Teach your children, in accordance with their age and stage of development, how to release their painful emotions fully and completely, while still taking others into account and not hurting anyone.

How can you do this?

Here are a few examples:
- Go for a walk in the woods and yell at the top of your lungs until you get tired.
- Make an "anger notebook" and write in it all of the difficult emotions.
- Hit a punching bag until you calm down!
- Watch a sad movie and cry in order to let the sadness out of your body.
- Draw or paint what you are feeling and describe your work's details.
- Breathe slowly: inhale and exhale slowly several times, until you experience calmness and serenity.

I hope that you enjoy reading this book together with your children. May your life be full of joy, satisfaction, serenity and love.

Na'ama Gal

Contact information:
naamagal4@gmail.com

And finally – A special gift…

Feeling Hearts

Here you will find heart pages with pleasant and unpleasant feelings.
You are invited to help your children cut out the hearts, or use them as stickers.

Here are a few wonderful ideas for activities with the hearts:

1. The children will tell you of something that happened to them, something they dreamed about, or something they heard. After, they will draw their story and paste an emotion next to each figure.

2. Your kids and you will make up a story together.
   Draw the story together and paste a corresponding emotion next to each figure.
   Note: The figure can be a person, animal, object, plant, still life or an imaginary creature.

3. The kids and you will prepare an emotions notebook together. The kids will draw a beautiful cover page and write their names in it.
   After that, the children will paste a heart with a certain emotion on each page. According to the pages in the notebook, the children will learn to identify what they are feeling and will be able to express it with a drawing or by talking about it. Further on, when the children will experience different things, they will identify their emotion about it, find the corresponding page in the notebook, and draw or write their experience in it.

Enjoy your "togetherness" and open talks which will bring you closer together, about how you feel, as well as about listening to your hearts.

Sincerely Yours,

Na'ama

You are invited to download the special gift

of Feeling Hearts Stickers.

Just type in your browser:

https://bit.ly/2XnZmjA

Or scan the QR barcode:

Pleasant Emotions

Excitement

Affection

Appreciation

Confidence

Enthusiasm

Joy

Love

Serenity

Curiosity

Forgiveness

Hope

Gratitude

Caring

Pride

Relief

Admiration

Lightness

Satisfaction

Enjoyment

Gratification

Cheerfulness

Unpleasant Emotions

Disappointment			
Shame	Agitation	Stress	Sadness
Apprehension	Longing	Guilt	Fear
Concern	Anger	Embarrassment	Confusion
Fright	Revenge	Insult	Tiredness
Boredom	Disrespect	Regret	Remorse

www.ingramcontent.com/pod-product-compliance
Lightning Source LLC
LaVergne TN
LVHW072130060526
838201LV00071B/5005